Lessons
FROM MY TWENTIES
by MARQUITA BRADLEY

Copyright © 2014 Marquita Bradley

Scripture quotations are from the New Revised Standard Version Bible, copyright © 1989 the Division of Christian Education of the National Council of the Churches of Christ in the United States of America. Used by permission. All rights reserved.

ISBN-13: 978-0-9909314-0-9 (Paperback)

ISBN-13: 978-0-9909314-1-6 (eBook)

ALL RIGHTS RESERVED. This book contains material protected under International and Federal Copyright Laws and Treaties. Any unauthorized reprint or use of this material is prohibited. No part of this book may be reproduced or transmitted in any form or by any means, electronic or mechanical, including photocopying, recording, or by any information storage and retrieval system without express written permission from the author / publisher.

Published by G.G. Publishing, LLC

Dedication

This book is dedicated to my incredible parents, the Rev. Jeremiah and Martha Bradley. I will forever be grateful to God for your example, unconditional love, and unwavering support.

Mom, know that I will always cherish the wife, mother, sister, and friend you are. I pray that I am a fourth of the woman you are, as you are my *shero*. No one can ever replace my "Martha Jane." I love you!

Dad, words will never be able to express how much I miss you. I believe you are smiling down on your baby girl. Know that this one is for you. I hope I've made you proud.

Acknowledgments

God, I thank you for this opportunity to share some of my experiences with the world. You created me for such a time as this and I am grateful for the holy boldness to walk in all you have called me to be. Forever your daughter.

To my bestie Regine, you are the kind of friend everyone needs in their life. Thank you for being the Gayle to my Oprah. This is our year sis!

Thank you to my sister-friend Shakiria Howie! Without you this book would not have gotten completed. Thank you for your support, encouragement, advice, edits, and love throughout this process. I pray it returns to you 100 fold.

Dana Bly, I thank you for turning my thoughts for my book cover into a work of art. You are so gifted and talented! Elton Anderson you went from being a stranger to an instant friend. Thank you for my amazing photos! You are an incredible photographer.

Ariel Jackson I will forever be grateful for our friendship and your sense of fashion! Thanks for pushing me out of my comfort zone. You were right!

Thanks to Karen Abdul, Jennifer Freeman, Donnie Garner, Dacia Lewis, and Claudia Jean-Baptiste for taking the time to read my book in its early stages and give me candid feedback. I LOVE you all!!!

To all of my spiritual mentors, I thank you for your prayers, wisdom, guidance, love and support. I am grateful.

To my biological sisters Farena Bradley and Belicia Reaves, Thank you for your love and support. Bradley girls forever!

To my village of friends, sorors, and family who continue to support all of my endeavors, thank you. I may not have written your name individually, but please know that I value and appreciate you all.

Table of Contents

Dedication 3

Acknowledgments 5

Table of Contents 7

Introduction 11

Lesson 1
Faith 13

Lesson 2
Communication and Emotions 23

Lesson 3
Friends 29

Lesson 4
Knowing When to Speak 35

Lesson 5
Operating In Your Purpose............................ 41

Lesson 6
Love 45

Lesson 7
Pain and Sorrow... 51

Lesson 8
Counseling is for Everyone......................... 57

Lesson 9
God is AMAZING!!! 63

Lesson 10
Give Roses While People Can Smell Them 67

Lesson 11
God's Got Me... 71

Lesson 12
There is Power in Waiting.......................... 75

Lesson 13
If God Said It... 79

Lesson 14
Gifted to Serve 83

Lesson 15
Self-Reflection 87

Lesson 16
Traveling is Good For The Soul 91

Lesson 17
Getting to Happy 95

Lesson 18
Called 99

Lesson 19
Your Gut Never Lies 103

Lesson 20
In All Things Give Thanks 111

Introduction

On April 11, 2013, I started my countdown to 30 (I know, I know, thirty is the new twenty). While reflecting on my 20s, it was on my heart to share twenty lessons learned with my friends and family on Facebook. After seeing the great response and reflections from those closest to me, I decided to write what I hope is an inspiring, and somewhat comedic book elaborating on these lessons. Of course there were many more lessons learned, but I'll just stick to my 20s theme for now.

As I went through different challenges and experiences in my 20s, I would talk to those older than me to gain a little wisdom or just to make sense out of my life. I remember always hearing them say, "Oh, everyone goes through that," or "Yes, the same thing happened to me." My initial thoughts were, "Really? Why didn't you warn a sister?"

Take the quarter-life-crisis phenomenon, for instance. I had never heard about the quarter-life-crisis, until I found myself in the middle of one. While people often say, "Oh, yes, everyone goes through a quarter-life-crisis, no one really talks to you about how to get through it. It's rare to find someone who says, "Hey, here are some things I experienced during my quarter-life-crisis and this is what I did to work my way through it." So, in addition to sharing my personal experiences and the tidbits that have made me the woman I am today, I want to provide encouragement and, hopefully, some sound advice to others on navigating their 20s and beyond.

I often joke with my friends and tell them, I feel like people go through a midlife crisis when they don't take enough time to go completely through their quarter-life-crisis. What I mean is, that by really getting to know who you are as a person, understanding your goals, values and mission and then developing a plan to boldly pursue those endeavors in your late twenties can alleviate so many issues by the time you reach your forties. There is a saying "YOLO," which means You Only Live Once. However, 'once' will be enough if you live it right. If you're doing all you should be doing, everything you want to do and what your heart desires, then you can achieve your best life.

We all have issues we must work through and it's perfectly fine to come to a point where you ask, "Why am I here?" What is my purpose in life? What am I doing to figure it out?" The key or the "secret" to remember is that no one has it all figured out. We're all in this together, trying to discover who we are, what we were created to do, and our life's purpose. Hopefully, this book helps as you go through or simply reflect on your journey. I pray you all are blessed, inspired and get a few chuckles while sharing in mine!

Lesson 1

Faith

I have taken many leaps of faith in my 20s, all due to my faith in God, His word over my life and the fact that He NEVER fails. I had to learn that not everyone will understand God's calling for me or the necessary choices I had to make. I couldn't allow myself to believe in the fears of others over my faith in God. Sometimes all you have is a word from God and a promise to hold on to for dear life. By faith I learned that is all I need. Besides, without faith it is impossible to please God! #WaterWalkingFaith

When I was a little girl my father taught me the importance of believing God. I remember one day after church we were in the car and he told me to think of something I wanted God to give me. Like most children I loved candy, so I immediately said: "a Kit Kat." He said, "Ok, make sure you believe He will do it." I was so excited I could barely contain myself. I didn't know how, but I was convinced that God was going to give me a Kit Kat. That evening our family decided to go to the movies. While at the snack counter with my dad getting popcorn and drinks, the manager came up to the register and asked me what I wanted. With a huge smile on my face I said, "a Kit Kat." He reached down and handed me a king-size Kit Kat and said, "My gift to you." I couldn't believe it! I looked at my dad and asked if he had anything to do with that and he said, "No."

I learned two big lessons from that experience. First, my only job regarding faith is to believe God; the "how" is up to Him. And second, God will always do exceedingly and abundantly above all that I could ask or think. Here I was expecting a regular-size candy bar and yet I received a king-size. Though this was something small, I was still so excited to see God show up and show out even in the little things.

Throughout my life I've made choices, all on faith: to move across the country, quit a successful job and to completely change careers. I have a confidence and boldness to move forward on things regardless if anyone else sees or believes in my vision. There's a joke in my family that before I make any big decisions I call my mother to ask for her advice, only to do the opposite of whatever she says. Now, this is not to be disobedient or that I don't value my mother's opinion. I just know when it comes to big decisions regarding her "baby" she speaks from her fears of what could happen. I have to push past her fear, my fear and the fear of others to pursue the calling on my life. Others not understanding my choices does not discourage me because they are just that – MY choices. God gave ME the vision and no one else. While this faith journey has not been easy, it is totally worth it! I'm happy to report that my faith has now rubbed off on my mother! She now tells me to do whatever I feel led to do as it's worked for me thus far.

There were several pivotal moments in my 20s where I just had to step out and trust what God told me. I remember a time about two years after I graduated from college, when I was completely depleted and dissatisfied with life. I was not happy in my job, felt like I was slipping into depression and living in the shadow of the mundane life. I would just go to work, go home, sleep, cry, eat and repeat the next day. I felt unfulfilled and that something was missing from my life. Tired and ready for a change, I gave God five cities and said, "As soon as you release me, to whichever one, you know I will go there." About six months after He and I had that conversation, I got an answer. Yet, there were still things I needed to learn and get from the situation I was in. This is another little tidbit. Whenever I'm in a situation and I feel like "why am I here?" or, "God why don't you just deliver me?" I try to shift my thinking toward what it is I need to learn from the situation in order to be released to the next stage.

I finally got the urge in my spirit to move to New York City. Now mind you, I never wanted to live in New York City. I thought it was dirty, filthy and just too fast paced for a southern girl like myself. Being the daddy's girl that I am, I called my dad to talk about my decision to move. As we were talking he said, "Oh, your aunt lives there. I'll see if she wouldn't mind you staying with her." He called her and she said it was ok (thanks Auntie!). I immediately turned in my two weeks' notice and quit my job. No job in sight in New York and yet I still moved. Now, I'm sure you can imagine, most people told me I was crazy. Everywhere I turned someone was saying, "Oh my God, you know you don't have a job, you're leaving a very large fortune 500 company," or, "I can't believe you're doing this." However, it was more important for me to follow what God said, than to stay in a miserable situation just for a paycheck. So I went to New York, which ended up being one of the best decisions of my life. Now the first three years of living in the Big Apple I absolutely hated it and wanted to leave. I thought the city was overcrowded, dirty, extremely busy, and just a different vibe to the southern charm I had grown accustomed to. Without fail, every time I would try to leave there would be some big miraculous thing that would happen. I got offered a new job, found a church, and a new apartment all in a matter of three weeks in New York City. This reminded me of God's faithfulness and encouraged me to stay even longer. In hindsight I'm sure it all worked together in transitioning me to my current purpose and career.

Another big New York moment happened when I was about twenty-six years old and working as the marketing manager at a major non-profit organization. I again found myself in a place where I was just not happy. I'm one of those people who does a lot of self-reflection to discover why I'm feeling a particular way. There was still a void that was present and I felt like I wasn't living life to the fullest in terms of who I am and what I could be offering and giving others. Basically, I was not walking in my purpose. I continued to go through this stage, working at the non-profit, where I was just miserable.

This season actually introduced the cycle of what happens when you stay in a place longer than you're supposed to. Often this "depression" tries to seep into your mindset making you anxious and frustrated every day because you're out of place. That's a sign that you're not where you're supposed to be. So I continued talking to God and saying, "I gotta get out of this place." God was clearly working everything out on my behalf behind the scenes. There were several changes going on in the company. My current boss and I were having several issues and I was let go with a nice severance package. This is another little tidbit: we never want to move ahead of God. I wanted to quit this job 6 months prior, but a co-worker told me to just wait it out and trust God. Waiting those few months allowed me the time to save money, reduce my expenses and begin to strategize on discovering my purpose while not having to worry about finances.

    I decided that I wanted to allow my gifts to make room for me. At first I thought about becoming an actress. I started to immerse myself in all things creative. I bought books, started taking acting classes, and went to seminars. You name it, I tried it. I said, "Jesus I'm talented! Let me do this." Not that God ever really needs me to help Him work things together, but I gave Him something to work with. Upon greater reflection, I see it was just a setup and preparation for where he was about to take me.

    I was riding on the train one Sunday morning and met a woman who was a member of my sorority. We began to have small talk and then she invited me to an event she was producing at the Apollo Theatre in Harlem. I told her I would do my best to make it and thanked her for the invitation. A few associates and I decided to attend. I arrived at the event and there were so many powerful women in the arts and entertainment industry. I was so excited to be in the midst of such greatness. That event opened my mind to the possibilities of what I could do in the entertainment industry. The panel included a woman who was a casting director. She, along with the other women on the panel, talked about their experiences in the entertainment industry.

When living a life of faith, it is imperative to know that there are no coincidences. Every encounter has a divine purpose in the grand plan of your life.

Soon after that event a friend of mine invited me to another gathering. Upon my arrival I realized it was the same casting director from the event at the Apollo Theatre. I gave her my contact information and said, "If you need any help or anything, just let me know." Sure enough, two weeks later she called me and asked if I was available for an internship with her company. I thought, "I am twenty-six years old, I have my own place, I got my own bills… and all of a sudden I become an intern again." So you can just imagine how people were laughing at me saying I was out of my mind. There I was, "good and grown" and back at square one. Are you starting to see a trend here? You know my mother was praying to God because she didn't know what was going on with her baby. It's kind of crazy when you think about it. When I say I was interning, I mean working for nothing, nada, zip. But, I just continued to say to God, "I want my gifts to make room for me."

Those two key moments, leaving my stable job and taking an internship at a casting office, changed everything in my life. I was determined to trust and believe that God was going to open doors for me. Taking the step to go and intern at twenty-six years old I believe expanded the trajectory of my life and aligned me with my God given destiny. Through my internship I went from doing one film to casting and helping with multiple films and on to becoming a freelance casting director on television shows. I don't believe I would be where

Faith

I am now if I had not taken that leap of faith when God told me to leave my job and allow my gifts to make room for me. Stepping out on faith allowed me to discover gifts, talents, and passions I never knew were locked on the inside of me. I discovered a love and passion for casting and working behind the scenes in television and film. I also think God had to take me through different seasons to shift my dependency to Him rather than a paycheck. It amazes me how people thought I was irresponsible and unstable for leaving my job and depending on God when they depend so much on a corporate job. Corporate jobs will let people go in a heartbeat, leaving them flat broke within two weeks (just ask anyone who's been furloughed), whereas God has an unlimited supply of resources and never leaves us. So often people get attached to the resources and not the source, the one who is supplying those things–God. So for me, I'd rather stick with Him, as He is the "well that never runs dry."

I believe that in just taking leaps of faith, the rewards are endless and limitless. That is not to say it's going to be easy because it's not, but nothing worth it ever really is. It really allows you to finally discover who you were truly created to be. Once you uncover that, you continue to go from level to level in becoming an amazing person.

That's why the Bible clearly says in Hebrews 11:6, "without faith it is impossible to please God." I make it my mission every day to try and please Him by having faith in all that He has spoken over me, in me and about me. I stand firm in my belief that He is not like man that He should lie (Numbers 23:19). You have to be fully persuaded that God will do what he said, knowing that whatever He said has to happen. I don't want to sound like a cheerleader, but it's true. You have to believe it. You must have faith not only in yourself, but also in the God who created you.

Lesson 2

Communication and Emotions

I read a book titled *Crucial Conversations* by Kerry Patterson (a great read I might add) when I began working for General Electric. This book completely changed the way I communicated with others. In the book, the writer expresses that people rarely respond to what you actually say, but more so to the story they've created in their minds about what you've said. Now it has taken YEARS for me to understand and apply this in my own life, however, it has been so life changing! #SayWhatYouMeanandMeanWhatYouSay

In a time of sub tweets, subliminal messages, and online posts, I've learned to communicate effectively, stating exactly how I feel or my thoughts on a particular subject.

There are so many circumstances or factors that can impact the way people process what you're saying. Understanding that many times people may not respond or hear what you're actually saying is vital. Clearly articulating your perspective in a respectful, yet direct manner, helps remove some of the guesswork and confusion around your message. This applies in all relationships, with friends and family, and certainly in the work place. Understand that many times people are not responding to or hearing what you are actually saying, but to the things that are going on in their own mind. Again, it has taken time, but I've really learned to be very clear and concise in all of my communication. Most folks are NOT direct in their communication and will often try to push their "storylines" on you, but you must refuse to get tied up in their emotional web. Indirect communication is not healthy or productive and it really just opens the door to unnecessary drama.

As women, we often tend to say everything is "ok" when we know it's not. If someone hurts your feelings, just say that. If you don't agree with something someone has said about you, say, "Actually, I don't agree with that!" If you don't appreciate something, find time to gather your thoughts, collect yourself and then tell them that you were offended by the comment and for it to never happen again. This works better than just saying, "It's ok," and going with the flow. It always amazes me that when men are pretty direct they're seen as being strong or as leaders. However, when women who are pretty direct are often seen as being controlling, aggressive or worse—being perceived as the "B" word. That only means you know who you are, and you are not afraid to express that. Being able to effectively communicate in all of your relationships will surely save you lots of time, headaches and heartaches.

Forming good communication habits and cultivating emotional stability will help strengthen your overall confidence and decision-making. A lot of times we are told, especially when we're younger, not to let our emotions control us. So we grow up trying to suppress them. My advice would be to go through your emotions. I wouldn't say go around people, for instance, if you're feeling down and out or having a bad day. I try to seclude myself to prevent spreading negativity around, but I let myself feel those emotions. I come back around others once I have finally regrouped and had time to deal with the issue. Then I move on.

Dealing with negative emotions is a significant skill that you will probably have many opportunities to practice in your 20s. You know the negative emotions right? Sadness, feeling

Communication and Emotions

overwhelmed, anger, hurt, frustration, pain, heartbreak, just to name a few. By no means have I mastered or remedied the occurrence of the dreaded "bad day" or any negative emotions. However, there are a few key things that I always try to remember when they come up:

1. It's ok to embrace how I am feeling
2. I have dominion over my emotions
3. I will not make major decisions based on temporary emotions or situations.

Emotions and communication go hand-in-hand. Giving yourself time to get mental and emotional clarity will allow you to communicate better with others.

Interestingly, I have also found that expressing positive emotions may present some challenges. For example, have you ever known someone who has a hard time saying, "I love you," or, "I appreciate you?"

In my 20s, I really got into the habit of verbalizing love and appreciation to those around me. I feel like people genuinely want to know they're loved, needed and even desired. So saying, "Thank you," or a simple, "I appreciate you," helps to bring reassurance. Most people will not deny a positive affirmation and being able to effectively communicate and express those will enhance both personal and professional relationships.

Your communication skills and emotions will definitely go through a refining process in your 20s. The changes and challenges however, are worth it as they help you mature. By the time you hit thirty, you will know your truth and will not be afraid to speak it if you do the work now. You won't be entrapped by what other people think because you know you have a good heart and your communications and emotions are all coming from a great place. When you function as your true self, people tend to respect you more. If they don't, they remove themselves from your life leaving room for God to place the right people in your life!

Lesson 3

Friends

So many lessons learned on this one! I must admit that I have been blessed with some amazing friends! However, I know many people who have struggles in this department. The saying, "People come into your life for a reason, season, and lifetime," is not just a cliché! Discerning which category folks fall in to will save you so much time and heartache in the long run. God has a plan for your life and as harsh as it may sound, not everyone can go where He is taking you!!! You can delay God's blessings when you try to hold on to people once their season has passed in your life. Thank God for the friends who are still there and become family. It's very rare, so be sure to cherish those friendships, and let them know they're appreciated. #FriendsAreChosenFamily

    When it comes to friendships, I feel like I have seen it all. I think some of the biggest lessons come from those who you think are lifetime friends and you realize they were really just for a season. When people show you who they are, believe them!! A woman I use to work with would always say, "You're not special, you're next." What that means is if you see a "friend" treating other people a certain way, talking about other "friends" negatively and just behaving in a manner you know is not appropriate towards others, don't sit and wait around thinking you're special. It's only a matter of time until this is going to happen to you.

    I think one of the biggest lessons for me was that my life's purpose didn't start to take off until I let some people go. Whether they are relationships or friendships, you just have to step out on faith and release those things that are not for you. Sometimes they are weighing you down and you are not able to soar. You can't be the eagle God has called you to be when you're clucking with chickens. Many times when people are like, "Oh, I'm so hurt," or, "I'm so stressed," there is an underlying issue. They are simply not releasing the things God is trying to get them to move on from. Whether that's a job, people or whatever, we must understand when seasons have changed.

I'm so grateful for the lifetime friends God has given me who have become family. It's so rare, which is why I try to make it my business to cherish those friendships. In your early 20s, you're probably thinking, these are my friends from college, and they'll be here forever. Then you realize some people just take different paths. Not everyone is going the corporate route, the entertainment route, etc. Not everyone has the same values or goals. People you may meet along the way may show you one thing today and, due to life's circumstances, they change. Each change starts to chip away at the very essence of who you knew them to be. When this happens you need to reevaluate your friendship.

It's also important to reevaluate who is making you an option in their life and not a priority. When you notice that you're the one always calling, you're the one trying to make it work, and putting in the effort, then you know it's time to make a change. You have to say to yourself, "I'm valuable and I'm bringing much more to this friendship than I'm getting out of it." Know for certain that if the friendship is not elevating you or helping you to progress, it is actually pulling you down.

One of the most important lessons to learn is how to identify God-ordained friendships. This will help you to differentiate those who are there to teach you lessons for a certain period of time and those who are there for the length of the journey. Pray and ask for discernment. You will then discover you are living a more fulfilled life. That doesn't mean letting go is going to be easy, and it doesn't mean it's not going to hurt, but treasure the memorable moments and know it will be worth it. You will be able to move forward knowing that if God is taking something away from you, then He's either going to replace it with something better or make it so that you don't even miss that thing or person.

In this culture of "BFF's", you must know that everyone is not your best friend forever. Value your friendships. Live, love, laugh. Travel together, get to know them, but don't be so quick to call any and every one your friend. No Ma'am! Some of those people will hang out with you today and won't even speak to you tomorrow, yet the title is thrown around so loosely. You can't afford to carelessly allow just anybody into your inner circle. Attaching yourself to people without knowing their plan or destiny is like getting on the wrong train and going nowhere fast. They say you can tell where you're going by the five people you spend the most time with, so hopefully God is one of those people and the other four you're choosing carefully.

Lesson 4

Knowing When to Speak

Early in my 20s, when I thought something I would say it whether someone asked me for my opinion or not. Over the years, I've learned to use wisdom and discernment before sharing my opinion. Sometimes people just want to be heard or to vent! Just because it comes to my mind does NOT mean I have to share it, LOL (laughing out loud). Take heed…This will assist in not having unnecessary arguments with your loved ones and friends. Now when you ask for my opinion, know that I will give it to you straight! #BeReady

    With effective communication, also comes a need for the gift of discernment, as I talked about in an earlier chapter. Over the years, I've learned that you have to use wisdom in knowing when to share. This provides the greatest chance that people will be able to receive the message that you're trying to give. You don't want people to discredit your message or what you're trying to say just because of the manner or timing in which it's being said.

    Within my set of friends, I was often seen as the mother of the group. I didn't always like that, but I accepted it. Some of my friends would get into…let's just say, very interesting situations, but would not tell me until after the fact. Not because they wanted me in the dark, they just didn't want to hear what I would have to say about those "interesting situations." There were also friends who would come to me before making decisions or getting into predicaments because they needed to hear the truth, the whole truth, and nothing but the truth. Just being a friend and finding a balance between knowing when to listen and when to extend advice is often key.

Lessons FROM MY TWENTIES

As I got into my late 20s, I started to just be that listening ear and sounding board, if needed. To this day I'm constantly asking my friends, "Are you telling me this because you want to vent or do you really want my opinion?" Getting clarity in the beginning helps me know how to proceed. For the venting friend who just wants to be heard, I allow them to go ahead, and get everything off of their chest. I chime in to let them know I hear what they're saying and understand why they may be feeling a certain way. It doesn't mean that I agree with them, but it acknowledges that I hear what they're saying. Now, if they ask for my opinion or advice, then I give it, but within the communication and emotional maturity of "my truth."

Probably the number one situation that will pull on your communication discernment is friends and their relationships with potential mates. For me this is a real challenge, because my friends are so much like my family. If I see them in horrible and destructive relationships it is extremely hard for me to just sit back and watch in silence. However, we all have to make our own choices. I've learned that I can't want more for people than they want for themselves. If they're happy and content in that place, then it's not my position to constantly tell them, "No, you should leave him, girl…he's not right." No. Clearly, after a while they have to get to a point where they want more for themselves and make decisions in line with that desire.

Ultimately understanding when to speak boils down to wisdom, timing, self-control and intention. Wisdom is key to communication because it will inform and prepare you to

Knowing When to Speak

know the time of when to speak; give you the power of self-control to not speak solely from your emotions; and focus your mind so that the intention of what you say is communicated clearly.

When the timing of your speaking is correct it will position your words for greatest effectiveness. Self-control will preserve you emotionally and will help establish accountability. Lastly, intention is the purpose for your speaking at all. It can be measured by the result of what you are trying to communicate. Do your words harm or do they heal? The goal is to make sure your intentions align with your actual delivery.

Forming good habits around when you speak will help you alleviate some unnecessary arguments with your friends and family.

Lesson 5

Operating In Your Purpose

I've had a few jobs in my 20s and even made a career change between the ages of twenty-six and twenty-seven. I've learned that sometimes we stay in jobs longer than the Lord intended. When you are operating in your purpose there is a certain grace that is over your situation. Once it is time for you to leave and you continue to stay, frustration begins to set in. Soon things you used to laugh off become annoying or all hell breaks loose and you're wondering what happened. Sometimes God will allow you to get frustrated out of a situation to move you to the next stage of your purpose. The key is to identify these things early on and move with God instead of running behind Him. This will NOT be EASY because He doesn't show us the entire plan, but it IS WORTH IT! Knowing that He already has a plan for our life, it is necessary to tap into that plan and walk in His Will! #PurposeDriven

There have been several books written on purpose and destiny. Some of them are great tools in assisting you on your journey to discover who God created you to be. However, I've learned the best way to learn the purpose and true intention of something is to go directly to its creator. We spend millions of dollars on self-help books in our country mostly because we don't take the time to go to our creator to see what He had in mind when He created us. Everyone has a purpose and destiny in life. Spending time with God will allow you to grow deeper in Him. This will ultimately begin to unveil what His desires are for your life.

Sometimes we get so complacent and comfortable in certain situations that were only intended to be temporary. God will send people, signs, and confirmations that it is time to move on, but we delay because of fear. This causes the very thing you prayed for to turn into a hindrance and ultimately disobedience. You are no longer operating in your purpose because your seasons have changed and yet you are trying to remain the same. Try wearing your wool coat, sweater and knee boots on the 4th of July in Los Angeles, California. What once was a source of warmth and comfort could ultimately kill

Lessons FROM MY TWENTIES

you in the wrong season. Learn to obey God and MOVE! I've learned to identify my seasons and move with God regardless of how I'm feeling at the moment. He has GREAT things in store for His children. Trust your Father.

Lesson 6

Love

"Lawd Jesus, it's a heartbreaker!" I've had my share of them in my 20s. While I couldn't see through the tears at the time, I grew so much from my past relationships. Honestly, they taught me more about myself than anything else. They taught me what my non-negotiables are and that it is fine not to settle in life or in love. I learned that as outspoken as I am, I'm capable of submitting to a man when I'm confident of his ability to lead. Another huge lesson was that just because someone is a great guy doesn't mean he's **MY** great guy. I could settle with any guy and rush to get married or wait for the man God has chosen to walk with me in my purpose. Clearly, I chose the latter. #GodsGotMe

Love. So, I have had my share of all sorts of relationships in my 20s. Ranging from the "Oh my gosh, I think he's the one," to the, "I think he's a good guy, but I'm not sure." Of course who can forget "Mr. Right Now." And "He is definitely NOT the one." None of them worked out for me, but they taught me so much about myself. Your 20s are a good time for you to explore, re-examine the things you thought you could tolerate and refine the infamous list of "must haves" in a future mate. You know the list I'm talking about right? The list of him being tall, dark and handsome LOL! Just checking. While there are no guarantees that you will get everything on your list, the process behind realizing what you want and which things are significant to you is necessary.

One of the greatest pieces of advice I received on relationships is to always ask myself, "If this person never changes, would I be ok with this person forever?" Many times we go into relationships thinking they will be better, or he could change. My friends and I like to call him Mr. Potential. The thing about falling in love with Mr. Potential is the fact that he indeed has the "potential" to do great and wonderful things, but he also has the potential to do nothing.

Mr. Potential is loaded with talent, ability and intellect that could lead to amazing things… or NOT. Women often fail in their 20s trying to submit to men who have no vision, no sense of direction and who are completely lost. You get frustrated trying to make them into what you see, though they can't see it for themselves. One thing you can't give a person is ambition. Waiting on the untapped potential to unfold could again be a hindrance to your personal development. It's all about finding someone who has a vision coupled with a plan, who can truly be a leader for you and your family. We have to be careful and intentional about whom we submit to and allow to lead us. Our destiny depends on it.

A great guy does not mean he's my guy. That understanding helped me navigate dating and relationships in my 20s. I have a lot of great male friends who have laid the foundation of what a great guy is and how I should be treated. I also had an amazing father who unconditionally loved my mother until his last breath. So I have seen what love looks like, and I know it's possible, therefore, I choose not to just settle for a "good" guy. I believe God has someone specifically for me. Now, that doesn't necessarily mean that everyone has a specific person. I just believe that God does have certain individuals that he divinely connects for a greater purpose or mission.

So, don't think you're missing the boat. Don't think, "Why not me?" Use this time in your 20s to get to know who you are. Many people will rush into marriage in their 20s, only to divorce in their 30s. Trust that the right time will be your time. Maximize singleness in your 20s by getting to know who you are, what you like and dislike, what you can tolerate and not tolerate, and the things you need to improve in yourself. Use the time to become the woman you want to be. Then when you do meet your mate you're completely whole, not searching for something within him to complete you. And yes, I do think you can be completely whole in Christ prior to meeting your mate. I don't subscribe to the "better half" belief as I think it is better when two whole individuals become one (not 50/50).

When you find your wholeness in Christ you will be a compliment to him instead of looking for him to come in and complete you. Personally, I have chosen to walk in my purpose while waiting for the man that God has for me. I am excited to meet him soon. Try not to worry because yours is on the way!

Lesson 7

Pain and Sorrow

Though often recited, I've discovered that time does NOT heal all wounds or pain. However, God, prayer, and time grants you the gift of managing or coping with pain. One scripture I came to appreciate is Psalm 30:5, "…*Weeping may linger for the night, but joy comes in the morning.*" #TheJoyoftheLordisMyStrength

The year was 2006 and I remember being so excited for my first trip out of the country. My friends and I were young, free, and fabulous, so we decided to backpack across Europe. I flew home to South Carolina the week before my trip to spend time with my father who was in the hospital at the time. One year prior to this trip, we found out my dad had cancer. He was supposed to have surgery that August to remove all of the cancer cells from his bone marrow. The week before his surgery he got pneumonia and was admitted into the hospital. The doctors cancelled the surgery, as his body couldn't handle the operation given the pneumonia. It was now November, and my father was still in the hospital. I truly wanted to see my dad before I left the country, so my boyfriend at the time, decided to fly me home to SC from NYC instead of North Carolina to spend time with him.

Once I got to South Carolina, I spent the first two days in the hospital with my dad singing and talking to him. After the first few days I went to my parent's home in Cross, South Carolina. I'd spent so much time packing and preparing that I had not spent as much time as I would have liked with my dad. I felt horrible. I was at the hospital with him before I was

Lessons FROM MY TWENTIES

leaving for my flight and I told him, "I'll just stay here with you and go on my trip another time." He told me to go and have fun, since this trip was something I'd been dreaming about for years. I asked if he was sure and he said, "Yes." I gave him a big hug and a kiss on the forehead before leaving to catch my flight back to NYC.

Two days later my friends and I were off on our adventure. Our first stop was in London where we stayed with a dear friend from college. When I phoned home I was elated to find out that after three months of being in the hospital my father was home. I cried tears of excitement and pure joy! This was one of the happiest moments of my life! It's what we'd prayed for and I couldn't believe how strong he sounded. I told him I loved him and couldn't wait to see him.

My friends and I enjoyed London and went on to spend about two days in Italy. While in Italy I got the feeling that I needed to call home to check-in. Over the next two days that feeling got stronger and stronger. We had already checked out of the hotel room so I had to wait until our next city before I could call home. Next up on our journey was Paris! When we arrived at our hotel that night the front desk guy kept yelling in French and saying I needed to call my family. Clearly I couldn't speak French and could barely understand what he was saying. My friend was translating a few things to me but, I could tell she wasn't saying everything. We rushed into the hotel room and I called my mom to see if everything was fine, it wasn't. My father had passed away in our home two days ago prior to the call. Words can't begin to describe the pain, sorrow and utter devastation I felt. I'm tearing up just writing this now. Everything after that moment was a blur. My amazing best friend Regine Jean-Baptiste somehow figured out how to get me back to the states and home to South Carolina to be with my family. My life would never be the same.

I've always heard that the Holy Spirit was a comforter and for the next few years I experienced his presence firsthand. As a Christian many people tried to comfort me with scripture or typical quotes like, "God doesn't put more on you than you can bear," or, "He's in a much better place now." While all of that is true, it didn't ease the pain from the great loss I experienced. Silence really can be golden. In times when you don't know what to say, just allow your presence to speak for you. Just let people know you are there should they need a shoulder to cry on. Too often people try to ease their personal discomfort of feeling helpless in how to assist a person in unspeakable grief by doing or saying things they don't need to. I wish some of those people could have read my chapter on communication and learning when to speak. There are some things, places, hurts and pains that only God and He alone can heal.

Respect the process of dealing with grief, knowing that everyone copes at different paces, in various ways. This experience allowed me to know God in a deeper and more personal way. I am forever grateful that in the midst of pain, there was still a lesson learned.

Lesson 8

Counseling is for Everyone

Never be afraid to seek help. #TrueWholenessComesFromGod

After going through the tragedy of losing a parent, it took a while before I was able to adapt to my new life. I was now fatherless. I tried to be strong for my mother who lost her husband and best friend, as well as for my sisters who were now without a father and friend. I was so concerned about my family that I was in denial about how deep this loss had really impacted me. I turned to food and began to eat my pain away. I felt abandoned. My superman had found his kryptonite and it was cancer. He died. I woke up so many days and said, "I guess he's not coming back." This was all such a horrible nightmare and each day reminded me that it was now my reality.

So many dreams I had as a little girl died with my father. I thought my dad would live to give me away at my wedding. In fact, I remember playing him the song we would dance to during the father-daughter dance the year before he passed away. Who was going to walk me down the aisle now? I did not want to think about marriage anymore. All of those fantasies went away now. To think about the actual wedding day would just remind me that my father was gone.

Lessons FROM MY TWENTIES

The depth of the pain from the loss of my father changed my entire makeup emotionally, spiritually and mentally. You see, grief can create a modified and possibly unrecognizable you. I knew that I was different. I mastered putting on a smile for others, because very few people understood what I was going through. It was difficult to take advice from people who still had their dads to call. Who could deal with the weight of what I was carrying?

After year two my pain was definitely seeping through the mask of my smile. I remember my best friend suggested I speak to a counselor. Now, at the time I thought of the many stigmas associated with speaking to a therapist. I told her I was fine and did not need to speak to anyone. I was wrong. The truth is I had so many mixed emotions regarding my faith, the grief, and the feeling of abandonment I felt that I simply did not know where to begin. I would schedule appointments with counselors, but never show up. I was ashamed and embarrassed. Therapy was not something discussed openly in my circle of friends at the time. I battled with grief internally for three years following the loss of my father, before I finally took the step to actually go and see a therapist. This was one of the most liberating decisions of my life. I found someone who patiently allowed me to talk, cry and sometimes just sit my way to healing. It was an hour once a week to discuss everything I had been through. We also established a plan on how I could start to move forward. As I mentioned earlier, many of my dreams died with my dad, but through my counseling sessions I learned that I just needed to dream another dream. Things would be different. I was different...and that was ok.

Now, I want to be clear that my support system was amazing. I love my family and friends dearly, but sometimes we need a fresh set of ears, eyes, and skills to help us break through. I am grateful for my counselor and her amazing couch! Looking back, I realize that going to counseling was the beginning of me stepping into the direction my life is in today. I was able to get to the root of my pain, and deal with the issues of abandonment, emotional disconnection and feeling disappointed that God did not allow my father to remain on the earth with me. I found some sense of closure in not understanding it all and being at peace on this new path. Counseling was good for my soul. Without it, I am not sure I would have reached wholeness in my heart and growth in my walk with God. I am now a firm believer that counseling is for everyone. If more people talked it out, we would have more healed individuals, families, and a much better world. #WholenessIsYourPortion

Lesson 9

God is AMAZING!!!

My limited vocabulary cannot begin to express how grateful I am to have a personal relationship with God. He is faithful!!! #GetToKnowHim

I'm seriously in love with God. After losing my earthly father I got to know God as Father. My relationship with him has grown so much throughout my 20s. Like any relationship, if you want to get to know someone intimately you have to spend quality time with them. I had to learn to not just go to God with my lists of wants and requests, but sit and listen to what's on His heart. It was through intimacy that I found peace, love and unspeakable joy. Life is filled with many challenges and the ONLY way I have made it through is because of my relationship with Jesus Christ. He corrects me when I'm wrong, celebrates my wins, comforts me when I'm down and pushes me to do more than I ever thought was possible. He has taught me forgiveness, grace, mercy, and what unconditional love is truly all about. He has provided me with an amazing family, a wonderful example in my parents, health in my body, protection from dangers seen and unseen (joyrides with strangers, relationships with those who didn't know him, etc.), friends who have become family, and a true appreciation for who He has created me to be.

I'm so elated to know that ALL things work together for my good. Regardless of your past, know that it's never too late to receive God's love and grace. He cares about every aspect of your life. Your only job is just to believe Him.

Lesson 10

Give Roses While People Can Smell Them

We tend to celebrate people when they can no longer receive the praise. I'm a big believer in telling people how much they mean to me while they are still here. Everyone wants to feel appreciated, loved and heard. Be sure you let those in your life know these things daily. Don't take it for granted. So I wanted to take this time to celebrate my "BFF" Regine Jean-Baptiste! She is an amazing woman of God who exemplifies every essence of the word "friend." Through the years we have laughed, cried, prayed, danced, shopped, traveled, cheered, shouted, sang, argued, comforted, dreamed, believed and so much more with each other. I'm so grateful God blessed me with a friend for all seasons. She's the Gayle to my Oprah and I love her dearly!!!! #BFF

    When you are young there is an unspoken feeling that you will live forever. While we never say this, it is often reflected in our actions. Especially now, with the popularity of YOLO (You Only Live Once) and songs that say to "party like it's the last night of your life," you feel like you have all the time in world in your 20s. The reality is none of us knows how long we have on this earth. It is rare that we express to our friends and family how much they mean to us.

    Recently my heart was saddened to hear about the death of two young bright actors who committed suicide. While I'm sure they were both adored and LOVED immensely by their friends and family, I wonder how many times they were told they were loved. How many times did someone call, not wanting anything but, to check-in on how they were doing and to let them know that they mattered? When my father passed, I wondered if he truly knew how much I LOVED him. Of course I told him every time we got off the phone, holidays, his birthday, etc., but I wondered if there was more I could have done to express my gratitude for who he was in my life. That experience has helped me in communicating with friends and family just how appreciative I am of their love, support, and for who they are in my life. Don't wait until tragedy is at your door to give roses to your loved ones. The time for celebration of life is always now.

Lesson 11

God's Got Me

Life isn't fair but the knowledge that God reigns over the just and the unjust gives me peace. Oftentimes when people mistreat us we try to take matters in our own hands. I've learned that when God says, "Vengeance is mine…," (Romans 12:19) He means it! I pray for those who come against me, for they know not what they do. I'm a child of the King and know that my father LOVES me unconditionally. Don't walk around thinking you can treat people any kind of way. Not God's children! "We know that all things work together for good for those who love God, who are called according to his purpose" (Romans 8:28). #Chosen

There is so much comfort in knowing that God is God all by Himself. Although we often have our own plan for our lives and how things should work out, life rarely marches to the beat of our drum. Regardless of what situation I may put myself in or the enemy may try to send my way, I know that God is with me. Sometimes we try to control every area and situation in our life because there is a trust issue rooted in the belief that "if I don't do it, then it won't get done." While that may be what people say, God is waiting for us to release EVERYTHING to Him so He can have His way in every area of our life. We must learn to surrender to His will because He has an even greater plan. This is difficult for some in normal, everyday living and it becomes even more difficult when we feel there is an injustice done towards us. Sometimes we try to justify our malicious actions because of how others treat us. It is written in Psalm 110:1, "Sit at my right hand until I make your enemies your footstool." Trust and believe that the same people who mistreat you will reap what they sow. Additionally, they don't even know that they just became a step for you to go higher. A simple smile and thank you is sufficient when this happens. It's a sure sign you are going to another level.

Lesson 12

There is Power in Waiting

Believe it or not there is power in waiting. Great things come to those who receive their blessings at the appointed time. #GotPower

    Living in a "microwave" generation can make us believe that everything we want or desire should be available in an instant. This flawed thinking often leads to a lack of character development and maturity needed to sustain fulfilled dreams. The waiting process, while sometimes frustrating and uncomfortable, brings power, wisdom, strength and so much more to your life. This lesson is not something that comes easy in your 20s. Especially, when you've spent most of your schooling preparing to take over the world or been raised to go to college, get married and live happily ever after…in short order.

    Pacing yourself in your 20s can pay off huge for you down the road. One powerful element in waiting is the time you allow yourself to discover your purpose, identity and heal from things that may have negatively impacted you. Think in terms of relationships. Say you meet a great guy but, you haven't healed from your daddy issues, and he hasn't healed from his issues with mom. We then have two hurting people attracted to each other's brokenness. So, what happens once you get healed and no longer live under the weight of those issues? Are you still equally yoked? Waiting until both parties are healed and whole will result in a more sustainable relationship and marriage.

Waiting and pacing can work the same way for you professionally. In my 20s you couldn't tell me I didn't know how to run every department at my job, better than the current manager. While innovation is an amazing gift there is something to be said for having wisdom and experience. I really believed that I had prepared enough to go from the classroom to running the boardroom. Little did I know, my learning was only beginning. Waiting is often seen as something people do in a passive sense. I would encourage anyone who is in a waiting season to make the most of the time and view it as a gift. Always learn as much as you can and work on becoming the best version of yourself. Prepare for the place you want to go and wait for the Lord to equip you with the essential tools needed to maintain that position or relationship when you receive it.

Lesson 13

If God Said It

If we can endure the process of waiting, then we will, without fail, experience the fruits of our waiting. Always know that if God said it, it's already done! #DelayisNOTaDenial

I've always known that I would one day be a woman of Delta Sigma Theta Sorority, Incorporated. So when this didn't happen in my college years I had some serious questions for God. I heard Him clearly say that I would be granted this desire of my heart, yet it didn't happen when or how I wanted it to. This happened in a few areas of my life. I planned and did everything I was "supposed to" and still didn't get the promotion, job, or whatever else you chose to fill in the blank. I've learned to stand firm on the Word of God! It's never about if He can or will do something, but about knowing it will surely come to pass if God said it.

As I mentioned before, there is always a lesson to be learned in delayed blessings, whether it's strengthening your character or teaching you patience. It may be that it's just not your time YET! So, let us not grow weary in doing what is right, for we will reap at harvest time, if we do not give up (Gal. 6:9). On April 20, 2008, God made good on His word to me by fulfilling a dream in allowing me to become a member of Delta Sigma Theta Sorority Incorporated! I am forever grateful for this blessing!!!!

Lesson 14

Gifted to Serve

Sometimes (really most of the time) the thing that bothers you the most is the thing God has gifted you with the ability to serve as the solution. Often times we just complain about the problem instead of offering our services to those who are clearly not operating in excellence (or their purpose). So the next time something is aggravating you and you notice that you're the only one who's aggravated, it's probably something you're called to do. #YourGiftsArentJustForYou

      Have you ever attended an event and noticed the many things that needed to be improved? Did you just complain or offer to lend a hand? Often times there are situations and circumstances where we are either agitated or frustrated with things that seem to not bother others. This is what I call being gifted to serve. There is a reason why you are the only person upset at the event that starts late, the customer service not being up to par or whatever the case may be. You are called to allow your gifts to make room for you. This means instead of always getting upset, you should be moving into action to see how you can contribute to making that "thing" better. Our gifts and talents are not solely for our own personal advancement. We have to know that everything is so much bigger than us. We have to stop being consumed with our own issues and problems to be the solution for someone else's.

Lesson 15

Self-Reflection

I tell folks all the time, "We lie loudest to ourselves." Honest self-reflection allows you to assess who you are versus who you THINK you are. It allows you to deal with the only person you can control...yourself. #LoveWhoYouAre #

Early in my 20s I learned to reflect on the person I was and the person I wanted to be. I've always been pretty honest with myself about my strengths, weaknesses, personality, etc. For example, I embraced the fact that I am a loud lady (yes, we do exist) and my laugh is even LOUDER! It's a part of what makes me...well, ME! However, I've had to work on other things that I didn't like about myself. Sometimes it's hard to face the truth about certain traits, characteristics or mannerisms we see in the mirror. Oftentimes we try to point out the flaws in others to suggest they are the reason we react in unfavorable ways, but honestly we can't blame others for why we behave a certain way.

No one should have that much power or control over our emotions or behavior. Ask yourself the tough questions to get to the root of your issues so healing and true transformation can take place. Growth is a journey, not a destination. Strive to be a better version of yourself every day. Once you do the work in yourself, you become more compassionate and understanding of others who have yet to do the work. This does not excuse bad behavior, but it does allow you to see beyond the surface.

I've also found it very freeing to deal with my personal issues. You start to love yourself even more, understanding you are a work in progress. It's cliché, but true, "You may not be where you want to be, but thank God you aren't where you used to be." Cheers to you for moving forward!

Lesson 16

Traveling is Good For The Soul

One of the greatest gifts you can give a child is the ability to see the world beyond their town, city, state or country. There are so many wonderful places to explore. Traveling teaches you what's really important in life and how to discover true happiness. #TravelingBelle

Ever since I can remember my family and I always took vacations. Growing up I thought that's what every family did during the summer or around the holidays. What I thought was as a small gesture from my childhood turned out to be one of the best gifts my parents gave me. Traveling exposes you to other cultures, allows you to bask in the beauty of God's creation, to gain an appreciation for the freedoms we have here in the United States, and shows where we may have missed the value of what's really important in this journey called life. There's something special about being able to connect with people even if you can't understand a word they speak. I always knew the world was so much bigger than my small town and I've been blessed to see that first hand.

Living in New York City, I was amazed at how many people had never visited another borough let alone another state or country. We must instill these values and share these opportunities with our youth. It's the gift that keeps on giving. Those life experiences coupled with education is something NO ONE can take away from you. It opens your mind to what you value in life. How is it that some of the poorest people around the world have so much joy? We have to get away from focusing on our own situation to see that our lives are so much bigger than we think. There is a world waiting for us to walk in all we have been called to do. Scripture says in Romans 8:19, "For the creation waits with eager longing for the revealing of the children of God." How much longer will you make them wait? What will it take for you to start your business or blog, to write your book, sing your song, or find the cure for cancer? You get it right? It's time to answer the call of your destiny.

Lesson 17

Getting to Happy

It's your party and you can cry if you want to. #JoyIsYourPortion

Early in my 20s I thought I had my life all planned out. I was going to get my MBA, own a marketing firm, marry well, have twins and live happily ever after. I remember working at an ad agency and thinking, "There must be more to my life than making million dollar companies richer."

I worked at a non-profit and I still didn't feel like I was living my best life. During this time I started to seek the Lord for His will for my life. I wrestled with the question of what happens when your plan doesn't align with God's plan for your life? I'll tell you what happens…you surrender. I did just that in March of 2010. I simply gave God a "yes." I told the Lord that I wanted my gifts to make room for me. It was a turning point in my life. I never felt so free! Not only was I happy, but I experienced and continued to experience pure joy! I found my purpose, and walked in it every day. It took courage and faith to step outside of what society says is the "formula" to life in order for me to truly live.

We have to get to a point where we pursue our own happiness instead of living lies to appease others. It is ok to change courses at any point in life or chart a new path. This is where breakthroughs and miracles happen. I won't say that it will be easy or that you won't have to overcome any obstacles, but I will tell you that the rewards far outweigh anything the enemy may try to throw your way.

So, no I don't have my MBA nor do I own a marketing firm, but what I do have are God's plans and desires for my life. Let me tell you that they are exceedingly and abundantly above ALL I could ask or think!!! #SheWon #Blessed #Happy #GodsGirl...P.S. The hubby and babies are in Gods plan!

Lesson 18

Called

In my early 20s I would often say, "Don't go where you're tolerated, go where you're celebrated!" I thought it was ludicrous to be around people who did not appreciate you or what you bring to the table. While I still feel this way at times, the truth is, now I go where I'm called whether folks like me or not. I've realized that my life is so much bigger than me and I may have to sacrifice my comfort in order to do God's will. #HisWillisWhatsBestForMe

The Bible never states that you will be comfortable in all that God calls you to do. I think it is a big misconception to think that while you are walking in the will of the Lord, everyone will be happy and excited for you or cheering you along the way. This simply is not true. The enemy knows that you are a person with an incredible assignment and so he assigns people to try to aggravate and irritate you out of your position. In my mid-20s, when I wasn't happy with something I just left. I didn't feel the need to be in situations where people didn't get me or what I had been called to do. The Lord began to show me that some of the very people who were giving me a hard time were my assignments. I kept running if I wasn't celebrated, but God began to teach me about what it means to be called.

Think about what would have happened if Jesus left every place where they didn't "accept" Him or "celebrate" His arrival. We wouldn't have our dear Savior, as it was His mission to complete His assignment regardless of what people said, believed, or how they treated Him. We have to understand that God knows all and start to ask questions to gain wisdom on why we are in certain situations. Why am I in the office with the verbally abusive manager? Does he need prayer? Do I need to endure the crazy policies of the school principal in order to know how to pray for my students? There is a reason why we are where we are.

If we continue to seek the face of the Lord, He can direct and show us how, even in the midst of what looks like adversity, He will get the glory because we are called and chosen.

Lesson 19

Your Gut Never Lies

Always trust your instincts; it's the Holy Spirit's way of guiding you. #TrustandBelieve

In my last semester of college I started dating a guy I met at a local event in Washington, D.C. While he seemed to have everything one would want in a guy—handsome, educated, no kids, a career, knew the Lord, etc.—there was always a feeling inside me that something just wasn't right with him. I could never put my finger on why I felt this way but, the more time I spent with him the stronger this feeling in my gut grew. I remember telling a few friends about my hesitancy and they ALL said I was over-reacting and that he was a great guy. Needless to say I continued talking to this gentleman after my graduation in December of 2004 and he even came to see me in South Carolina during the Christmas holidays. I told my sisters about him but never mentioned him to my parents because I just wasn't sure where this relationship was headed.

We talked every day in January as I was gearing up to move to North Carolina to start my new job. I ended up having a week of training in Richmond, Virginia the first week of February, so "Chaz" and I decided to spend the weekend together, since I was only 2 hours away. Friday could not come fast enough. I was so excited to see him. My friend and I finished our last session early and we headed to D.C. for a weekend to remember!

"Chaz" came to pick me up at Howard's campus. We laughed and talked the whole way to Maryland. He had just moved in January from his place in Virginia and was telling me all about his new neighborhood as we got closer to his building. Once we were in his apartment we talked about our plans for the weekend. It was Super Bowl weekend so he wanted me to come with him to a friend's party. I told him that was fine and we would just chill on Saturday. I was a bit hungry from the trip down so we headed out to get something to eat. For some reason he really wanted to go to this place all the way in Virginia. Tired and hungry, I didn't want to fuss about his choice, especially since he seemed so excited. It took us an HOUR to get to the restaurant. Let me just say, there is nothing cute about a hungry woman! I was starving and very angry because we passed hundreds of restaurants to get to this place. Nevertheless, I was committed to us having a great time and a memorable weekend. We ordered, ate (the food was sub-par to say the least), and headed back to his place.

After an uneventful dining experience, I decided to end the night. Once back at his place we were both tired and decided we would turn in for the night. I took a shower and once I was out he did the same. We cuddled up on the bed. I exhaled. Soon our cuddling led to a mini kissing make-out session. He knew that I didn't have sex, as it was a personal choice of mine at the time. "Chaz" then got on top of me and held my hands together above my head. I told him to stop. I didn't like where this was going, but he didn't listen. Here I was with an ex-football player on top of me and his grip got tighter around my wrists. I started moving my body and yelling for him to stop, but he just kept kissing on me. He took one of his hands and pulled my panties down. I got my hands loose and started trying to push him off of me. He just kept saying softly and calmly in my ear "Just calm down, don't fight it, you know you want to."

I started to cry. All of the strength in my 165 pound, five-foot-five frame could not move this man off of me. He then tried to put his penis inside of my vagina. I crossed my legs and held them tight for dear life as this man tried to pry my legs open and forcibly penetrate me. After what felt like forever but was more like 5-10 minutes of him unsuccessfully ramming his penis on the outside of my vagina, he rolled over and told me to "quit acting like a baby." I laid there shocked at what just happened to me. I rolled out of the bed and crawled to the living room sobbing. I was SO completely embarrassed to be caught in that situation that I didn't call anyone right away. I immediately was reminded of all of the gut feelings that something was "off" with this guy. Never in a million years would I have imagined that he was capable of trying to rape me. I curled up in the fetal position, pulled my nightgown over my knees and cried myself to sleep. I didn't sleep long. I didn't know what to do to get out of this situation.

He woke up the next morning as if nothing had happened. I called my girlfriend who was still at Howard and told her I needed to come over today. She said it was fine and would wait for me to get there. What happened next still blows my mind to this day. "Chaz" comes in the living room and tries to hug me. I push him away of course, using a few choice words to say the least. I told him I just needed him to take me to Howard's campus and he wouldn't have to worry about me again. He said he didn't know why I was so upset but he'd take me wherever I wanted to go. I got dressed and told him I was ready to go. He says, "I guess you don't want to see me anymore," and I said, "You guessed correctly." He then asked me if I had everything and I told him I did.

    He opened the door for me and I walked out rolling my carryon suitcase. As soon as the last wheel crossed to the outside of his home he slammed the door and locked the top lock. Distraught was an understatement to express what I was feeling. I was put out *Diary of a Mad Black Woman* style; only this wasn't a movie but my life. How does an educated woman get herself into such a predicament?

    We all watch the movies and call the woman "stupid" and say what we would do in that situation but, let me tell you something, I did none of those things. I made my way downstairs, but I had NO IDEA where I was! I called my sister hysterically crying. I felt helpless. She calmed me down just enough to understand what just happened. After telling her I wasn't calling the police and that I just wanted to leave, she told me to knock on someone's door to ask for the address to the apartment building and a phonebook. Embarrassed and still in shock I knocked on someone's door to do as she said. A gentleman opened the door giving me a strange look as his lady was in the background. I asked him for a phonebook and the address to this place. He told me to hold on a second while he went to retrieve the book. As I waited, "Chaz" walked downstairs right past me as if I were a stranger and drove away in his car.

I mean if I wasn't already humiliated, this heartless act definitely pushed me over the edge. The guy brings me the phonebook and tells me the address. I thank him and sit on a chair in the lobby to look for a cab service to my friend's dorm. I'm flipping through the phonebook and can't find any listings for cabs. I begin to cry harder and tell my sister I can't find any numbers. She then tells me to look under taxi. I was so out of it at this point. I finally get a taxi to my friend's place. The entire ride I kept thinking about the feeling I had about "Chaz" all along. Why didn't I trust my instincts? I learned many lessons from that experience. One of the biggest lessons was that I listen the FIRST time to my gut. I don't need to wait around to see why I feel a certain way.

Throughout my 20s I have shared my story with friends. I have been shocked to learn how many women had similar experiences of sexual assault or who had been raped. Please know that you are NOT alone and it is NEVER YOUR FAULT. It took me a while to deal with what happened that night. I had to forgive myself before I could truly forgive him. What I know for sure is that at some point you will find yourself in a situation and wonder how you got there and how to move forward. Know that God is always there and he can heal you, restore you, and give you a new heart.

Lesson 20

In All Things Give Thanks

Turning thirty has really caused me to reflect on my past experiences, current path and where I'm headed. I must say that I am truly grateful for it all. It has made me stronger than I ever thought I could be; and happier to be living life and not just existing. I'm less judgmental of others (we're all trying to deal with things/life the best we know how) and more appreciative, as I know the true value of life and the time we have on this earth. I'm more loving, joyous, and most of all... ME! I'm grateful for the woman my 20s have shaped me to be and even more excited about all my 30s has to offer! So cheers to my 20s, and a warm embrace to the gift of entering my 30s. #GodsGirl #Blessed #Grateful #Thankful #FlirtyThirty #GodFavorsMe

I am beyond grateful to have made it through my 20s. There are so many friends, associates, etc. that didn't get to see their 30th birthday and I know it is God who has allowed me to see this day. I wrote this book simply because I wished there was someone who sat me down to tell me some of the lessons they learned so I could glean from their wisdom. I pray that something I've said has touched, inspired, or confirmed what you already knew to be true. Sometimes it's just refreshing to know that you are not alone and that others have shared similar experiences.

Know that there is healing in your testimony. We are all here for a reason. Someone is waiting on you to share your story. Once you know who you are in Christ and begin to walk boldly in the knowing that EVERY situation, circumstance, setback, hurt and triumph will work out for your good, it seriously only gets better from there. In my best *"Ms. Celie's"* voice from *The Color Purple*, "I's HERE!!!"

I can't wait to see how God shows out in my life as I continue to truly walk by faith into all He has destined for me. I am even more elated to see who you become once you start walking in your God-ordained path. It's never too late! So here's another cheer to you for living your life on purpose. You are equipped and ready. I love you all with the love of Christ! #It'sOurTime

www.ingramcontent.com/pod-product-compliance
Lightning Source LLC
LaVergne TN
LVHW021400080426
835508LV00020B/2372